11 REASONS
TO BECOME RACE
LITERATE

A Pocket Guide to a New
Conversation

Milagros A. Phillips

11 REASONS TO BECOME RACE LITERATE:

A Pocket Guide to a New Conversation

© Copyright 2016 by Milagros Phillips

info@milagrosphillips.com

http://www.MilagrosPhillips.com

Cover Design by Milagros A. Phillips

Cover Painting: AND THEN THERE'S SUNLIGHT

Milagros A. Phillips

2016 Acrylic on Canvas 30X30

Web Art Galleries: http://milagros-phillips.pixels.com/

TABLE OF CONTENTS

DEDICATION

I dedicate this small book to my children, for whom I want a better world, and to my parents, who made me believe a better world was possible.

ACKNOWLEGEMENTS

I wish to thank the following people for their help in creating this book and for their contributions to my inspiration: My courageous ancestors; my children who lovingly encourage me to create; my friend Doug Tanner, who during one of our conversations inspired me to write a couple of pages about why race literacy is important, an inspiration that culminated in this short book; my precious friends who support all my crazy ideas—Lisa Peters, Adrianne Eliseo for all the great questions and ideas, Deirdre Mcglynn; Susan Hadler, who took time out of her busy schedule promoting her new book, *The Beauty of What Remains*, to do first edits; Michelle Hanson, Author of *Ocean Oracle,* for sharing her experiences as a writer and her encouraging words; and my editor Leslie Lass, who deserves special thanks for her excellent work.

INTRODUCTION

Why is race literacy important? Why do we have to talk about things that happened hundreds of years ago? We need race literacy because, after hundreds of years of segregation, the country is still divided along racial lines. We need to have an awareness of race, the subtle biases it purports, and the way in which those biases affect the most simple of exchanges, from an exchange with the grocery store clerk- to the way a doctor speaks to his/her patients.

In one form or another race affects all people, regardless of the color of their skin. We need to understand what happened long ago because the affects of what happened are still with us today and because the history that clarifies those events has not been properly explored. We need race literacy because what we know and what we don't know affects our worldview.

Racial literacy is a phrase that is most often attributed to France Winndance Twine, an American sociologist and film maker, who studied interracial families in the UK, where one of the parents was of African descent. Her research found that in an attempt to teach their children to counter racism, these parents would train their children to recognize racism, to respond to it, and to defy it. Race literacy has taken many forms since the middle passage, from mothers having to tell their young daughters how to survive rape, to modern day parents having to train their sons on how to behave if they are stopped by the police when driving while black, to now a-days, walking while black.

In this book race literacy refers to the education needed by all citizens of the US as a way of knowing their country, their fellow citizens and themselves in the context of their citizenship. It is about demystifying race in America, and giving way to a new conversation. It speaks to the knowing of our collective history as a way of understanding each other and understanding race-based current events. And it refers to the use of race literacy to find new and creative ways of being together as one human family.

Race literacy helps us to be an emotionally and physically healthier society, it can give us a richer economy and it sets us free by filling in the blanks that keep us shackled to a five hundred year old past.

After more than twenty years of lecturing, facilitating seminars, and leading conversations on race, I have come to the conclusion that what America needs is a massive educational campaign aimed at retelling the American story. Alongside this campaign, we need to do the personal and individual work to support the transformation. This work is about us.

Year after year, I have seen how quickly people change their views on race when they are given the missing pieces to our American history, namely, the African American part. It's as if we all have small fragments of the whole story, and when we defragment (defrag) the information everything falls into place.

I was born and spent my formative years in the Dominican Republic (DR). As a small child I learned two very important things from my father. When we lived in the DR, he used to rig his radio to get his news from various parts of the world. He would listen to the BBC; Radio Free Europe; the US news; and, of course, the DR news. He always used to say, "Never get your news from one source." This helped me learn to defrag my world and to connect the dots. His favorite saying was, "You must learn to reason!" To him, this meant that nothing was random and that there was an order to everything. It was my job to find it. Connecting the dots helps us see the whole picture. We might do well to remember the words of Dr. Martin Luther King in his "Letter from a Birmingham Jail": 'Moreover, I am cognizant of the interrelatedness of all communities and states," he writes. "I cannot sit idly by in Atlanta and not be concerned about what happens in Birmingham. Injustice anywhere is a threat to justice everywhere."

When you see the whole picture you see how everything impacts every other thing in the web of life. When you see the whole picture, you can't believe in isolation or segregation anymore. All things and all people are somehow connected. When it comes to race, I have spent the last twenty five years connecting the dots, and helping myself and others, people of all backgrounds, become race literate.

Race literacy changes everything. I remember a conversation with an executive a year after he had attended one of my two-day intensive seminars. At that time the seminar was called "Transformation, Race & Healing" (its current name is "Race Demystified"). I had trained more than one thousand employees for his organization, including top executives and board members, and he said, "That seminar has changed everything in our organization. We don't even interview the same way anymore." This man had learned that, to have a better world for ourselves, we must make a better world for others. By securing our neighbor we secure ourselves.

Another man from the same organization said, "During our annual meeting we could tell who had attended the race seminar and who hadn't by the things they said during their presentations." In two days (the length of the seminar), people who had been living within a shell of misinformation were liberated by their newly discovered race literacy, and it changed the way they saw themselves as Americans. It also changed the way they saw their employees, the way they behaved in relationships with people they considered different from themselves, and the way they created growth opportunities for their employees.

I hope these pages will motivate you to find the information you need in order to understand this important topic we call "race." I also hope that you will find your place in this new understanding of race and that you will do whatever you are called to do—if only to raise the consciousness of those around you. Even if you choose to do nothing, at least you will be doing "nothing" from an informed place.

11 REASONS TO BECOME RACE LITERATE:

A Pocket Guide to a New Conversation

Study the past if you are to define the future. – Confucius

There are hundreds of reasons to become race literate... Here are 11.

REASON 1

RELIEVE STRESS AND FRAGILITY

While racism is not our fault, understanding it is our responsibility. And that understanding starts with race literacy. When I was a child, I used to hear my parents say, "If you want to hold people back, keep them ignorant." Race is one of those topics that makes people feel fragile, and that fragility shows up as anger, shame, resentment, guilt, anxiety, frustration, impatience, and a host of other fear-based emotions. Say the word "racism", and the emotions escalate to the point that people just don't want to talk about it. Without communication we just carry the emotions buried within us. Those emotions take center stage whenever something happens that is related to race.

Human beings are meant to connect, to become friends and to be good neighbors to one another. When we don't connect we carry a kind of grief that colors our lives, and unresolved grief becomes depression. If you don't think we are a nation carrying grief, just look at all the people who are on anti-depressants. Grief makes us fragile and stressed.

Conversations and the sharing of our experiences is vital to our race literacy and to the creation of community. When we come together to speak about our common legacy, we learn about each other. We establish relationships, which, if nurtured, can lead to trust; we grow as humans; and we enhance our knowledge of race. It lets us see how our experiences may be similar and different. It helps us be less judgmental and more compassionate towards the behaviors and experiences of others, and gives us a clearer understanding of our worldview. As we get to know one another, build trust, and become community, we become less stressed. When we are well informed we are less fragile, and we feel less threatened. When we feel less threatened we are more likely to engage in a productive conversation than when we are at a deficit. Race literacy is worth the investment of our time and energy.

REASON 2

AFRICAN-AMERICAN HISTORY IS AMERICAN HISTORY

Many Americans think that only African Americans were kept from their history. Most, if not all of the history of Africans, brought as free laborers to the "new world," was erased. These unpaid laborers were violently made to adapt to new religions, new diets, and even new ways of thinking. White Americans were being kept in ignorance as well. By omitting the history of everyone who was not of European descent, white Americans created a national identity based on a small part of their story. The part of American history that relates to human cargo for the building of the nation has not been given proper attention in the history books.

And when it has been brought up, it has been quickly shot down.

An example of this was reported by the Denver Post, September, 2016. According to J. Paul, one of their reporters, in Jefferson, Colorado, the school board wanted "to sweep 'under the rug' certain parts of the AP U.S. History curriculum" and wanted to promote "patriotic material, respect for authority, and the free-market system" while avoiding "civil disorder, social strife or disregard of the law." The upset students protested the impending censorship of their history curriculum. They exercised civil disobedience to make their point, and took to the streets in protest. People use civil disobedience because the law does not always equate to justice. Wherever this happens, citizens bring attention to the injustice through acts of civil disobedience; and do their best to change the law, as they did during the Civil Rights era. African Americans chose non-violence to bring attention to their plight.

Americans are used to civil disobedience; indeed, the country was founded on it. Remember the Boston Tea Party? - And what about the Revolutionary War? That war was pretty violent. We don't have a problem putting that into the history books. Yet the history books in Jefferson, Colorado, were deemed to be too negative because they covered subjects such as the US internment of Japanese-Americans during World War II, slavery, and the Civil Rights Movement.

Still, there is much about our history that did not make it into any of our mainstream history books. For instance, the Spaniards are credited with starting the transatlantic slave trade. They were sailing ships with human cargo from Africa to the Caribbean for one hundred years before the Mayflower landed on Plymouth Rock. It is estimated that 15 million people were taken from the African shores, and only 400,000 were brought to the continental US. The rest were taken to the Caribbean and to Central and South America with approximately 6 million out of the 15 million actually surviving the voyage. The horrific conditions on the transatlantic ships caused disease; some of the enslaved revolted, and if their captors ran out of provisions, the enslaved were thrown overboard.

King George III, who was the King of England during the American Revolutionary War (one of the first cases of civil disobedience in American history), was married to a black woman. "Queen Charlotte, wife of the English King George III (1738-1820), was directly descended from Margarita de Castro y Sousa, a black branch of the Portuguese Royal House." Her name was Queen Charlotte Sophia of Mecklenburg-Strelitz, and she was an abolitionist. Even before she married King George III, while she was still a young child, she was an activist. As queen, she tried to get her husband to abolish slavery throughout their entire empire, including the colonies (what is now the US). Charlotte, North Carolina, is named after her, as are Mecklenburg County, Virginia, and the Charlotte Islands.

Race literacy leads us to ask different questions. Some years back, while visiting The Queen's Museum in London, my friend and I came upon an exhibit of Queen Charlotte and King George III. While learning about their lives together, their fourteen children, and her love of music, as well as of the arts, I found that these two people became more human to me. In a whimsy, I turned to my friend and said, "I wonder if King George III was poisoned?" A few days after we had visited the museum, my friend in the UK watched a BBC TV documentary about King George III in which there was mention that while DNA testing had been conducted on King George III's hair, arsenic poisoning had been found. There are some historians who believe that the American

Revolutionary War was the first war fought in this country for the abolishment of slavery.

Enslaved Africans and their descendants helped build America. Their free labor created a great deal of the wealth that the country stands on today. One example is that of "the Jesuit priests," who in 1838 sold 272 of the slaves they owned so they could "secure the future of the premier Catholic institution of higher learning at the time, known today as Georgetown University," (*The New York Times*, April 16, 2016). Now comes the task of making amends.

All Americans share a common history. I often remind whites in my seminars that it's important to "know thyself," especially if you're going to do any type of transformation work. The problem is that if you have been misinformed about your country's history, then you don't know those you share the land with, and you don't know yourself within the true context of your citizenship.

As an educated nation, our country does all Americans a disservice when it leaves them ignorant about their past. It's a way of saying, "We don't think that you can handle the truth about our past," which is a way of infantilizing them. There is a level of spiritual growth and maturity that we deny people when we hide their past from them. To hold people illiterate is to make them vulnerable to myths and superstitions.

While we know that our racial biases are wrong, we don't seem to know what to do about them. And we won't know until we become literate on the topic of race in America. It's wrong to deny someone an education; yet, that's what we do every day to Americans when we make them think that African American history is an extra-curricular subject to be studied separately or is a subject to be studied when we get to college, if the school even offers it. The US is one country; segregating history does not change that fact. Americans have built their lives on a false history that keeps them separate from one another and that divides them along racial lines. This has many consequences, not the least of which is economic.

REASON 4

RACISM IS EXPENSIVE

Our false history, built on racial illiteracy, costs us. It costs us as a nation, as communities, and as individuals.

White Americans believe their success is due to their hard work and merit. No one would argue that Americans work hard; however, before they can do the hard work that enables them to "make it," they first need access to opportunity. What seldom gets mentioned is that access to opportunity and to the possibility of financial and other success is based on skin color. There are many people of color in this country who work two or three jobs and who have little or no time off. Despite their hard work, they have limited access to opportunities, which affects their possibility for financial success. There are many ways to hold people hostage; denying access is one of them.

The Cost of Racism

In his article "Racism in the U.S. Has an Enormous Price tag: States Lose Billions of Dollars Because of Income Inequality," Pulitzer Prize-winning journalist and best-selling author Nick Chiles writes in the *Atlanta Black Star* that a "report released...by the Center for American Progress [CAP]...quantifies approximately how much America's fastest growing states are losing in tax revenue because of systemic racism against African-Americans and Hispanics."

Highlighting state-specific data, he goes on to say that in Georgia "the average income for whites in 2013 was $43,764. For black residents the average was $28,272, while the average for Hispanics was $26,838. By CAP's estimate, eliminating racial disparities in income in the state of Georgia would gain the state an additional $3.8

billion in tax revenue and would boost the state's gross domestic product from $455 billion to $522 billion."

In a November 2013 report released by the Altarum Institute and funded by the W.K. Kellogg Foundation, we learn that "minority communities continue to suffer systemic discrimination that weakens the U.S. economy" and that closing the earnings gap between whites and minorities "would boost earnings by 12 percent, an economic windfall of $1 trillion, for a nation burdened by debt and an anemic job market lift gross." In another Altarum Institute study, *The Business Case for Racial Equity*, lead author Ani Turner also examines the impact of closing the earnings gap and says that "total earnings would have been 8% higher, and GDP $1.2 trillion higher, in 2011."

Differences in earnings are not the only problem facing employees. Trust is a major issue in professional relationships. After hundreds of years of segregation, men and women are brought together in work environments and are expected to have successful work relationships. But often those relationships are strained, and finding middle ground can be difficult with the racial elephant sitting in the middle of those

relationships. Discrimination lawsuits and employee turnover are also part of the cost of racism.

REASON 3

KNOWING ONE'S HISTORY PUTS THINGS IN PERSPECTIVE

Since the 1500s America has been carrying the stigma of a social and moral wrong and has been trying to address it with very little historical facts, bad science, and a lot of misinformation. So, rather than dealing with it as a nation, we resist addressing race when we write the history books, we resist addressing race when we make policies, and we resist addressing race in our conversations. As a result the legacy of racism persists.

Race literacy puts things in perspective. It gives us background and context. It reminds us that life is a continuum, passed on from generation to generation, and mandates us to rethink race. The race-literate are not paralyzed before a five-hundred-year-old problem; they are empowered to make a difference and know they can. They are willing to work individually and collectively to change what at the beginning seems insurmountable. Most of all they are aware of the power of the collective and know that working together can yield greater results.

REASON 5

WHAT WE DON'T KNOW CAN HURT US

John Elliot Bradshaw, a counselor who speaks and writes about addiction, recovery, codependency, and spirituality is the author of *Family Secrets: What You Don't Know Can Hurt You.* In it he refers to family members acting out of a secret (something that happened within the family that no one has shared with them), without consciously knowing what the secret is. While something that happened within the family has not been communicated, people still act out, or exhibit behaviors associated with the uncommunicated event. An example would be a family in which someone has committed suicide, but the next generation has not been told. The new generation learns quickly that you never ask about that member of the family. Yet there's an uncomfortable feeling, a kind of depression, sadness, and shame within themselves and the family that they can't really explain. All that the new generation has is partial truths, and bits of stories that don't add up to a whole picture. They do their best to frame their worldview with what they have, but what they have is limited.

Racism is a social wrong that we have inherited with bits and pieces of information and a lot of missing truths. Because of our illiteracy, we act out of our American racialized family secret. We carry the shame, anger, and frustration of our predecessors and continue to segregate along racial lines. While progress has been made, it's been slow and hard won. Although there isn't one single person today who can be credited with the inception of racism into our society, we are all responsible for its transformation. But how do we transform what we don't understand?

The first step to our transformation is to come out of denial. Denial of America's racial caste system keeps us trapped in it. When one becomes race literate, denial is no longer a comfortable place to hide. When we come out of denial we face our anger, our hopelessness, and our helplessness. We stop bargaining with the circumstances, telling ourselves that if we deal with the economic issue we will solve racism. There are many wealthy people, including Oprah Winfrey, who will tell you that's not the case.

When we are race literate we accept the reality of what is, and we engage with the problem from a new perspective. We are not muddled with fragmented pieces, and we are able to create new solutions and to find new ways of being with one another.

REASON 6

RACE IS AMERICA'S MORAL DILEMMA

Race is America's moral dilemma. How do we justify making opportunities available to some, while denying it to others? In order to become comfortable with that kind of behavior we have to somehow justify it. We need a compelling story that we can live with, one that alleviates the cognitive dissonance caused by our actions.

We tell ourselves that some people are undeserving, not bright enough, or that somehow they just don't qualify, and are therefore ineligible for our good paying jobs, descent housing, good schools, and even good healthcare.

As human beings, we have been thrown together in a country that is largely made up of immigrants to solve the problem of racism. Whether we just got here yesterday, our relatives came on a slave ship, or they arrived on the Mayflower, we belong to the same human family, and we are part of the same country. To quote Dr. Martin Luther King, "We may have all come on different ships, but we are in the same boat now."

Dr. King knew that, without an understanding of the moral dimension, his work on race in America would be doomed; moreover, he understood race as America's moral and spiritual path. So, he used the principles of unity, non-violence, and compassion as well as his love for humanity to enact changes that transformed a nation and that left a powerful mark upon the world.

The thing to remember is that we all have the power to change and to enact change in our world. Standing squarely on the principle of compassion, with the realization that we don't know what we don't know, we could humbly transform America. By being open to learning, we create the space within ourselves to have a new and expansive experience. And, if we let ourselves be present with all that is, we emerge bigger than the problem. At that point the problem no longer has us; we have it! We become sovereign over our five-hundred-year-old legacy.

Race is woven into the fabric and foundation of our country, and it has been a moral dilemma that has haunted this nation from its inception. Economics, race, and injustice have been from the very beginning inextricably tied. From the kidnapping of the first African to provide unpaid labor to the emerging nation, to the denial of employment, racial injustice and the economics of inequality have always walked hand in hand. But make no mistake, fixing the economic problem is a step in the right direction, however it doesn't change people's hearts. As a nation founded on the principles of equality, and freedom, we need to remember that we stand for justice; that we are members of the same human family, and that a high value needs to be placed on every human life.

REASON 7

RACE FEAR IS MORE THAN SKIN DEEP

African-American history happened on our soil. It is the history that undergirds this nation, and literacy about this history (or lack thereof) impacts everything from our birth to our death. Throughout our lives a spirit from the past quietly haunts us and it rears its head when we make policies about such things as housing, healthcare, education, employment, and even access to basic human rights. This spirit goes by many names and one of them is fear. We have an inherent fear of the topic of race, a fear that has been with us for generations.

An Interesting Side Note about Fear

In the article "Study finds that fear can travel quickly through generations of mice DNA," Meeri Kim of the *Washington Post* writes, "A newborn mouse pup, seemingly innocent to the workings of the world, may actually harbor generations' worth of information passed down by its ancestors." Kim also points out that "the study, published…in the journal Nature Neuroscience, adds to a growing pile of evidence suggesting that characteristics outside of the strict genetic code may also be acquired from our parents through epigenetic inheritance. Epigenetics studies how molecules act as DNA markers that influence how the genome is read. We pick up these epigenetic markers during our lives and in various locations on our body as we develop and interact with our environment."

The study found that mice who were repeatedly traumatized while smelling cherry blossom oil eventually acted as if they were being traumatized simply by smelling the oil; moreover, the researchers found that the following generation had an even stronger reaction to the cherry blossom oil than the mice who were originally traumatized. Even more compelling is the fact that the researchers found the same traumatic reaction in mice for six more generations, making it seven full generations of traumatized mice. We could say that the new generation of mice, were acting out of what Bradshaw might refer to as "the family secret," as previously mentioned in this book.

From studying survivors of the Jewish Holocaust, we know that trauma is passed on. This has been very true of Native Americans, and many tribes are engaged in historical and intergenerational healing as a way of recovering the lifeblood of their communities. In our discussions of trauma and abuse, we rarely mention that a human being cannot traumatize another human without hurting their own humanity. By the power of our connection and the Spirit that carries us through this lifetime, somehow we remember what we have done, and what has been done to us, even when we are not conscious of the details. Whether we are victim or perpetrator, fear gets passed on.

Race literacy is transformative. Many years ago, as I was walking across a parking lot, I ran into a man who had attended one of my seminars about seven months previously. After exchanging greetings, his voice got somber and quiet. "I wish my wife had been allowed to attend the company's race seminar," he said. "You see we were at a ball game last summer and my wife made a racial joke that a year ago I would have laughed at. This year, it made me sick to my stomach." As a white man who had become race literate, he could no longer tolerate what he once thought of as funny. He had a new perception of "us and them" and used what he had learned in the seminar to go from information to transformation. He had allowed the experience of the seminar to not only change his mind but to also touch his heart.

On the topic of what gets passed on through the generations, I am reminded of a line in the movie *The Help*, in which the main character, Aibileen Clark, played by actress Viola Davis, says, "We [meaning the black maids] raise them [referring to the white children they nanny] with all our love; yet, they still grow up to be just as racist as their parents."

REASON 8

IT GROUNDS US IN FACTS

My daughter's high school chorus teacher, an educated white woman with a college degree, told her students that, "The reason blacks sing better than whites is because they have more nasal passages." Beyond the terrible biology, how does it affect a student who is one of a few children of color in a school system, to be taught by teacher who is steeped in myths about African Americans? How did that myth affect those students, regardless of the color of their skin?

Without the background that race literacy affords, we are left on our own to have the same uncomfortable conversations over and over again.

We repeat the patterns of shame, guilt, anger, and frustration that are so familiar, and we end up victims of a never-ending past that seeps quietly into the background of our present, and continuously creates our future.

Race literacy informs us of simple things, such as the fact that all hair is protein. The texture of the hair (curly, straight, and everything in between) is formed by the shape of the hair follicle below the skin. Skin color is caused by melanin. According to *Wikipedia*, "Melanin is an effective absorber of light; the pigment is able to dissipate over 99.9% of absorbed UV radiation." The greater the concentration of melanin, the darker the skin, and the darker the skin, the stronger the protection against UV radiation. This fact speaks volumes about geography and human adaptability, but it does not determine other characteristics of human nature.

REASON 9

WE ARE HERE TO CREATE A BETTER WORLD

We create our worldview with the information we have in our environment, and with the information we are given. When we are misinformed, our perception of self and other is askew, and those who are misinformed are bound to mis-create.

I believe that as spiritual beings we are here to love, to connect, to collaborate, and to leave the world a better place for future generations. When we fall short of the mark, we hide in shame, avoid speaking about misdeeds, and blame the victim for our shortcomings. We are here to create a world we can all be proud of, a world that works for all of us.

A massive national education campaign is needed to awaken all Americans to their history, particularly the parts that bring up the feelings of inadequacy we feel when dealing with the topic of race. Hiding from these feelings puts us in a weakened position that renders us defensive and powerless to do anything about our situation.

The race literate are empowered and open. They are curious about others and are genuinely interested in us, as community. The race literate tend to be more authentic in their relationships with people of different backgrounds. They are the first to admit that they don't know what they don't know, and are more willing to ask questions. Their helpfulness is about asking what might be best for those whom they serve, rather than dictating their version of what a "good" situation looks like. They are excited about possibilities and look for solutions that are inclusive of all concerned. They realize that when a population has been marginalized for hundreds of years, equality does not add up to equity, and they look to achieve justice.

The race literate are able to walk in another's shoes, they value their own experiences with race and that of others. They are more relaxed in their interactions and their conversations about race, than those who have little awareness of what race literacy is about. They educate themselves on the topic and help raise the consciousness of those around them, just by being their authentic selves. They believe it's possible to eradicate racism and work on themselves and in their community to do so.

We are here to create a better world, when it comes to race there is much work to be done. The good news is that together we can achieve anything we set our minds to.

REASON 10

RACE LITERACY REMINDS US OF

OUR COLLECTIVE POWER

Race literacy is powerful because it brings us face to face with who we really are. It allows us to own our true ancestry: we are all related and we are all Africans. It restores our innate connection. It takes away the stigma of "us and them" and allows us to live as one human family - a healthier human family. It gives new depth to the question, "Am I my brother's keeper?" (Genesis 49). And it reminds us of where we come from, and knowing where we come from keeps us grounded. Race literacy restores our innate connection. It also gives us a new vision of who we are and therefore of what is collectively possible.

The Civil Rights Movement, would have never been as successful as it was, were it not for the people of all backgrounds who participated and collaborated for its accomplishment. The collective power of human thought, followed by human action is unstoppable. Who we are is pure power. Think of what we could accomplish as a nation when it comes to race. A race literate populous with the will to transform our nation, could change the world.

REASON 11

IT SETS US FREE

Then you will know the truth and the truth will set you free.
– John 8:32

Race literacy is liberating. It allows us to think, act, and understand issues of race in its true context. It gives us a more rounded view of the country in which we live. It gives us facts rather than myths. It removes some of the fear we have around engaging in a race conversation. It makes for constructive dialogue, leading to more enlightened and creative ideas on how to enact change. And it leaves us energized rather than depleted from always needing to hide from the subject. Race Literacy is empowering.

Race literacy frees us to have healthier relationships with one another. It removes some of our fears and keeps us from creating stories about people we don't really know, as sometimes happens when we have incomplete information. It helps us discern between the facts and the story we create to fill in missing data. It makes for greater productivity at work and expands our view of the world at large. It gives us the opportunity to know ourselves better as communities and as a nation. Further, race literacy allows us to rethink education, housing opportunities, and even health equity. And it gives us the opportunity to rethink the ways policies and laws could be hurting entire communities; it opens opportunities to rethink how we might transform our world.

CONCLUSION

Human beings are extraordinary. Alongside our violent acts and our greedy behavior, we also have an innate capacity for compassion and love. We care deeply and have the ability to change. When we work together we can accomplish great things. We will never heal segregation with more segregation. Unity, commitment, and race literacy are the best prescription for creating lasting change.

The benefits of race literacy are enormous, compared to the consequences. Benefits such as:
-An emotionally and physically healthier society
-Less race stress and fragility A richer economy
-More productive and happier employees

-A better educated populous A more equitable society

-Healthier cross cultural relationships

-A clearer vision of our past and present

-A deeper understanding of who we are as a nation and much more...

How we get there

If we are to look at ourselves as a human family, and take a page from domestic abuse cases where we have been successful at treating and reintegrating the family, we have treated both victims and perpetrators. A healthy society knows that both victims and perpetrators have work to do on themselves, while continuing to function as a whole and collective unit. They know that they, both, have to look at the history of their behavior, step out of their old patterns, deal with their anger and create new, healthier ways of being. In order to do that, they need support, both individual and collective support. We create support in our communities by building bridges of connection. We do it by having conversations, we do it by taking action to make things better, and we do it by asking what is needed, and a lot of the times we do this one person at a time.

We need the kind of education that leads to transformation, an education that informs the mind and touches the heart. Once transformed, we can collectively reinvent ourselves and invent new possibilities. What race literacy does is to remind us that behind every interaction there is a story. While we are not just our stories, knowing those stories and facing our past can lead to freedom.

REFERENCES

Allen, F. (2013, November 20). Racism costs U.S. billions every year. *The Final Call*. Retrieved from http://www.finalcall.com/

Bradshaw, J. E. (2010, April 1). *Bradshaw on: Family secrets: What you don't know can hurt you*. [CD]. John Bradshaw Media Group.

Chiles, N. (2015, March 21). Racism in the U.S. has an enormous price tag: States lose billions of dollars because of income inequality. *The Atlanta Black Star*. Retrieved from http://atlantablackstar.com/

Kim, M. (2013, December 20). Study finds that fear can travel quickly through generations of mice DNA. *Washington Post*. Retrieved from https://www.washingtonpost.com

King, M. L. K., Jr. (1963, April 16). Letter from a Birmingham jail. Retrieved from Stanford, The Martin Luther King, Jr. Research and Education Institute website: https://kinginstitute.stanford.edu/king-papers/documents/letter-birmingham-jail

Melanin. (n.d.). Retrieved April 26, 2016, from https://en.wikipedia.org/wiki/Melanin Nguyen, Vi-An. (2014,

January 20). 15 of Martin Luther King Jr.'s most inspiring motivational quotes. *Parade*. Retrieved from http://parade.com/

Nguyen, J. (2013, June 24). Speaking about Race: Paula Deen and the need for racial literacy. *Huffpost Media*. Retrieved from http://www.huffingtonpost.com/jimmy-nguyen/speaking-about-race-paula_b_3488507.html

Paul, J. (2014, September 22). Jeffco students protest proposed "censorship" of history curriculum. *The Denver Post*. Retrieved from http://www.denverpost.com/

Swarns, R. L. (2016, April 16). 272 Slaves were sold to save Georgetown. What does it owe their descendants? *The New York Times*. Retrieved from http://www.nytimes.com/

Taylor, T. (Director), & Columbus, C., Barnathan, M., & Green, B. (Producers). (2011, August 9). *The help* [Motion picture]. United States: DreamWorks Pictures.

Turner, A. (2015, May 28). *The business case for racial equity*. Retrieved from http://altarum.org/sites/default/files/uploaded-publication-files/WKKF%20Business%20Case%20for%20Racial%20Equity.pdf

Valdes y Cocom, Mario de (1995). The blurred racial lines of famous families. *Frontlines*. Retrieved from http://www.pbs.org/wgbh/pages/frontline/shows/secret/famous/royalfamily.html

ABOUT THE AUTHOR

Milagros Phillips has spent the last 25 years bringing race literacy to colleges, universities, national leaders, corporations, and non-profits with her historically grounded, race-based seminars and programs. She is a speaker, an artist, and freelance consultant, and may be reached at:

info@milagrosphillips.com

http://www.MilagrosPhillips.com

Artist Website: http://milagros-phillips.pixels.com/

Made in the USA
Coppell, TX
10 June 2020

27561137R00042